# DOCK·TOK PRESENTS

## The Good, the Dad & the Punny

### LOGAN LISLE

TEN PEAKS PRESS®
EUGENE, OR

Cover design by Bryce Williamson
Interior design by Peter Gloege
Mug design on interior pages © Rae Dunn

For bulk or special sales, please call 1-800-547-8979.
Email: Customerservice@hhpbooks.com

 TEN PEAKS PRESS is a federally registered trademark of
The Hawkins Children's LLC. Harvest House Publishers, Inc.,
is the exclusive licensee of this trademark.

None of the trademarks or brands mentioned in the jokes or included in the photos
are associated with Dock Tok nor are they to be considered as endorsing this work.

### Dock Tok Presents...
### The Good, the Dad and the Punny

Copyright © 2023 by Logan Lisle
Published by Ten Peaks Press, an imprint of Harvest House Publishers
Eugene, Oregon 97408

ISBN 978-0-7369-8819-3 (pbk.)
ISBN 978-0-7369-8820-9 (eBook)

Library of Congress Control Number: 2023931220

**Printed in the United States**
23  24  25  26  27  28  29  30  31  / VP /  10  9  8  7  6  5  4  3

# I have a fear of elevators.

## I'm taking steps to avoid it.

# TO THE GUY WHO INVENTED ZERO,

**THANKS FOR NOTHIN'.**

# I wonder what kind of doctor Dr Pepper was.

## A fizzician.

# Did you hear that the guy who invented VELCRO died?

**RIP**

# DO YOU KNOW WHAT THE FIRST RULE OF THE PASSIVE-AGGRESSIVE CLUB IS?

"NEVER MIND. FORGET IT—IT'S FINE..."

# Guess who
# I ran into on
# the way to the
# optician's?

**Everyone.**

# WHAT'S THE DIFFERENCE BETWEEN A PIANO AND A TUNA?

YOU CAN TUNE A PIANO,
BUT YOU CAN'T TUNA FISH.

# I don't trust stairs.

They're always
up to something.

# I HAD A GREAT CHILDHOOD. DAD USED TO ROLL ME DOWN THE HILL IN TIRES.

## THOSE WERE GOODYEARS.

I turned down
a job where
I'd be paid in
vegetables.

The celery was just unacceptable.

# THE PEOPLE OF DUBAI DON'T LIKE THE FLINTSTONES,

BUT THE PEOPLE OF ABU DHABI DO.

# The oldest computer was owned by Adam and Eve.
# It was an Apple with very limited memory.

Just one byte
and everything crashed.

# WHY DID THE SCARECROW GET AN AWARD?

## 'CAUSE HE WAS OUT STANDING IN HIS FIELD.

# "Do. Not. Touch."

That's gotta be an unsettling
thing to read in braille.

# HAVE YOU EVER TRIED ARCHERY BLINDFOLDED?

## YOU DON'T KNOW WHAT YOU'RE MISSING.

# Do you know what's coming but never arrives?

**Tomorrow.**

# I ASKED MY DOG
# WHAT 2 MINUS 2 WAS.

## HE SAID NOTHING.

# I just burned two thousand calories.

That's the last time
I leave brownies in the oven
while I take a nap.

# I'LL NEVER AGAIN DONATE TO PEOPLE WHO COLLECT MONEY FOR MARATHONS.

## THEY JUST TAKE MY MONEY AND RUN.

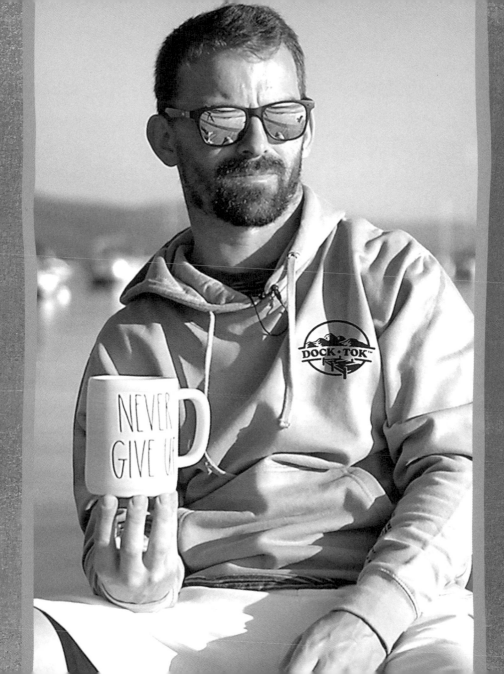

# What do you call two chiropractors who've got each other's backs?

Vertebros.

# I TOOK
# MY CAT'S MEDS.

## DON'T ASK MEOW.

# A man knocked at my door today.

**He asked for a donation to the local swimming pool, so I gave him a glass of water.**

# I'M WRITING A BOOK ON REVERSE PSYCHOLOGY.

---

## PLEASE DON'T BUY IT.

# If someone is ninety-nine pounds and they eat one pound of nachos,

## are they 1 percent nachos?

# I NEVER BELIEVED IN MY CHIROPRACTOR,

## BUT NOW I STAND CORRECTED.

# I wouldn't worry about your smartphone or TV spying on you.

**Your vacuum cleaner has been gathering dirt on you for years.**

# WHAT DO YOU CALL A MAN WHO CAN'T STAND?

## NEIL.

# I saw a microbiologist today.

He was much bigger than I expected.

# I'VE GOT TWO DOGS NAMED ROLEX AND TIMEX.

## THEY'RE WATCH DOGS.

# Sundays are always sad,

## but the day before is a sadder day.

# TWO WEEKS AGO, I SENT MY HEARING AID IN FOR REPAIR.

I'VE HEARD NOTHING SINCE.

# Whoever stole my copy of Microsoft Office, I will find you.

**You have my Word.**

# I USED TO HATE
# FACIAL HAIR,

## BUT THEN IT GREW ON ME.

# What state is known for having small soft drinks?

Minnesota.

# WHAT STATE IS KNOWN FOR HAVING THE MOST STREETS?

RHODE ISLAND.

# Why did the man fall down the deep hole?

**'Cause he couldn't see that well.**

# YESTERDAY I SPOTTED AN ALBINO DALMATIAN.

## IT WAS THE BEST I COULD DO FOR HIM.

# Why do some couples go to the gym?

'Cause they want their relationship to work out.

# WHAT DID ONE FLAG SAY TO THE OTHER FLAG?

**NOTHING—JUST WAVED.**

I wish somebody
could tell me
what "IDK" means.

Every time I ask, they say,
"I don't know."

# A SWEATER I PURCHASED WAS PICKING UP WAY TOO MUCH STATIC ELECTRICITY, SO I DECIDED TO RETURN IT.

THE STORE GAVE ME ANOTHER ONE
FREE OF CHARGE.

# I'm not a fan of elevator music.

**It's bad on so many levels.**

# A HISTORY DEGREE IS USELESS.

*THERE'S NO FUTURE IN IT.*

# I had to kick Cinderella off the softball team.

**She kept running away from the ball.**

# I KEPT WONDERING WHY THE BASEBALL WAS GETTING BIGGER.

## THEN IT HIT ME.

# I want to start
# a new diet.

**I feel like I have way too much
on my plate right now.**

# I'M MAKING
# A DOCUMENTARY
# ON HOW TO
# FLY A PLANE.

## WE'RE CURRENTLY FILMING THE PILOT.

# How does music say goodbye?

**"Audios!"**

# SOMEBODY RIPPED
# THE FIFTH MONTH
# OUT OF MY CALENDAR.

## I'M COMPLETELY DISMAYED.

In early spring,
gas prices will be
a dollar a gallon
just for a day.

April fuels.

# I HAVE A HEN THAT CAN COUNT ITS OWN EGGS.

## IT'S A MATHEMACHICKEN.

I just saw a burglar
trying to kick in
his own door.

He must have been
working from home.

# MY DOCTOR IS SO LAZY, I HATE IT.

HE'S DR. DOLITTLE.

# Dogs can't operate MRI machines.

## But cats can.

# DID YOU HEAR ABOUT THE GUY WHO EVAPORATED?

## HE'LL BE MIST.

# I have a disease—
# I can't stop telling
# airplane jokes.

**My doctor says it's terminal.**

# A FRIEND OF MINE GOT KIDNAPPED BY A GROUP OF MIMES.

~

THEY DID UNSPEAKABLE THINGS TO HIM.

# I couldn't quite remember how to throw a boomerang.

## But eventually it came back to me.

# WHAT KIND OF MUSIC DO CHIROPRACTORS LIKE?

## HIP-HOP.

# Know why I bring two pairs of socks when I golf?

Just in case I get
a hole in one.

# I NAMED MY DOG
# SIX MILES.

## THAT WAY I CAN TELL PEOPLE
## I WALK SIX MILES EVERY DAY.

# Did you hear?

## They're not making twelve-inch rulers any longer.

# WHY DID THE COACH GO BACK TO THE BANK?

TO GET HIS QUARTERBACK.

# Have you ever wondered how celebrities stay cool?

## They have a lot of fans.

# DID YOU HEAR ABOUT THE GUY WHOSE COFFEE WAS STOLEN?

## HE GOT MUGGED.

I saw a book yesterday that said, "How to solve 50 percent of all your problems."

So I bought two.

# I STARTED TELLING EVERYBODY THE BENEFITS OF EATING DRIED GRAPES.

## IT'S ABOUT RAISIN AWARENESS.

# Did you know that carrots make great detectives?

## They always get down to the root of the problem.

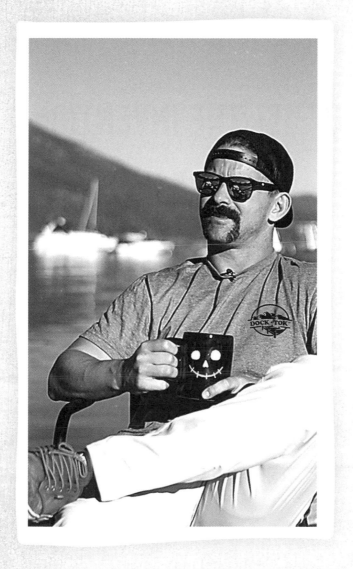

# OF ALL THE INVENTIONS IN THE LAST ONE HUNDRED YEARS,

THE DRY ERASE BOARD HAS GOT TO BE THE MOST REMARKABLE.

# Why is dark spelled with a *k*?

'Cause you can't *c* in the dark.

# I'M TAKING PART IN A STAIR-CLIMBING COMPETITION.

YOU'D BETTER STEP UP YOUR GAME.

# I used to work at a Pepsi plant,

but I left because it was
soda-pressing.

# I HAVE A BUNCH OF JOKES ABOUT UNEMPLOYED PEOPLE.

## UNFORTUNATELY, NONE OF THEM SEEM TO WORK.

# If a child refuses to nap,

## are they resisting a rest?

# A GUY TOLD ME
# A SHARK TOOK OUT HIS
# WHOLE LEFT SIDE.

———— 〰 ————

## I COULDN'T BELIEVE IT
## WHEN HE TOLD ME HE WAS ALL RIGHT.

# Do they allow loud laughing in Hawaii

## or just a low ha?

# I GOT FIRED FROM THE BANK TODAY. A WOMAN ASKED ME TO CHECK HER BALANCE. . .

## SO I PUSHED HER.

# Why aren't koalas actual bears?

They don't meet
the koalafications.

# MY FRIEND ASKED ME
# TO PICK UP
# 6 CANS OF SPRITE.

**WHEN I GOT TO HIS HOUSE,
I REALIZED I HAD PICKED 7UP.**

# MY BOSS ASKED ME WHY I GET SICK ONLY ON WORKDAYS.

I SAID, "I DUNNO . . . IT MUST BE MY WEEKEND IMMUNE SYSTEM."

# Never date
# a tennis player.

Love means
nothing to them.

I STAYED UP
ALL NIGHT TRYING
TO FIGURE OUT
WHERE THE SUN WAS,

AND THEN IT DAWNED ON ME.

# Why are mountains so funny?

Because they're hill areas.

# I'M CHANGING MY USERNAME TO "NOBODY."

**WHEN PEOPLE POST SOMETHING STUPID, NOBODY WILL LIKE IT.**

Did you know that there are more airplanes in the sea than there are submarines in the air?

Well, that's plane to sea.

# IF YOU DRIVE A SUBARU IN REVERSE, WHAT ARE YOU?

**U R A BUS.**

# What did the duck say when he bought ChapStick?

**Put it on my bill.**

# WHY DO SEAGULLS FLY OVER THE OCEAN?

~~~

**IF THEY FLEW OVER THE BAY, THEY'D BE CALLED BAYGULLS.**

# I had a dream last night that I was floating in an ocean of orange soda.

**It was more of a Fanta sea.**

# WHY DID THE BULLET
# LOSE ITS JOB?

## IT GOT FIRED.

# Did you hear about the claustrophobic astronaut?

He just needed some space.

# I JUST JOINED
# A DATING SITE
# FOR ARSONISTS.

## THEY SENT ME A LOT OF MATCHES.

I just got an award
for being the
most secretive person
in the office.

Can't tell you how much that
means to me.

# IN BRITAIN THEY USE A LIFT, BUT HERE IN THE UNITED STATES WE USE AN ELEVATOR.

I GUESS WE WERE JUST RAISED DIFFERENTLY.

# Did you hear about the ATM that got addicted to money?

It was having withdrawals.

# MY MOM COMPLAINS
# I DON'T BUY HER FLOWERS.

## TO BE HONEST,
## I NEVER KNEW SHE SOLD FLOWERS.

# Every time
# I get to work,
# I hide.

**Good employees
are hard to find.**

# I WAS AT MY FRIEND'S HOUSE, AND HE ASKED IF I'D SEEN THE DOG BOWL.

I SAID I NEVER KNEW HE COULD.

I can't believe
I got arrested
for impersonating
a politician.

I was just sitting around
doing nothing.

# I'M NOT WEARING GLASSES ANYMORE.

## I'VE SEEN ENOUGH.

# Last night my obese parrot died.

**It was a huge weight off my shoulders.**

# MY FRIEND ACCUSED ME OF STEALING HIS THESAURUS. . .

NOT ONLY WAS I SHOCKED, I WAS APPALLED, AGHAST, AND DISMAYED.

# WHAT always starts with a *w* and ends with a *t*?

## (It does.)

# DID YOU HEAR ABOUT THE RESTAURANT ON THE MOON?

## GREAT FOOD, BUT NO ATMOSPHERE.

# I would love to get paid to sleep.

That'd be my dream job.

# HOW WAS ROME SPLIT IN TWO?

## WITH A PAIR OF CAESARS.

# I got fired from the keyboard factory yesterday.

## I guess I wasn't putting in enough shifts.

# MY DOG ATE ALL MY SCRABBLE TILES LAST NIGHT.

I THINK IT'S GOING TO SPELL DISASTER.

**Yesterday
I went to a psychic.
I knocked on her
door, and she said,
"Who is it?"**

**So I left.**

# MY EMAIL PASSWORD GOT HACKED AGAIN.

## IT'S THE THIRD TIME I'VE HAD TO RENAME MY DOG.

# My doctor said
# I have the
# peekaboo virus.

**He sent me straight
to the ICU.**

# I HAVE TWO
# UNWRITTEN RULES:

1. _____
2. _____

# I'm never buying anything with VELCRO.

### It's a total rip-off.

# WHAT DO YOU CALL A MAGICIAN WHO HAS LOST HIS MAGIC?

**IAN.**

# Fun facts:

Did you know that every
odd number has an *e* in it?

# YOU WANNA KNOW WHAT THE LONGEST WORD IN THE ENGLISH LANGUAGE IS?

"SMILES." THE FIRST AND LAST LETTER ARE A MILE APART.

# When I found out my toaster wasn't waterproofed,

I was shocked.

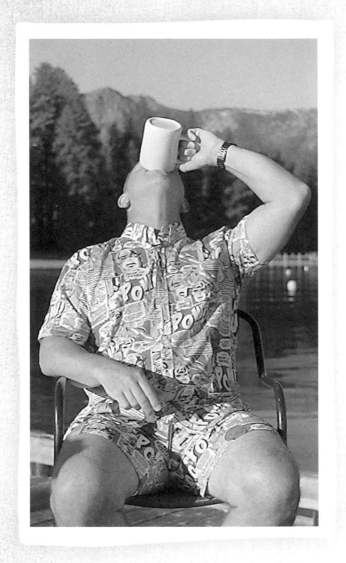

# I ENTERED TEN PUNS
# IN A CONTEST
# TO SEE WHICH WOULD WIN.

**BUT NOT ONE PUN IN TEN DID.**

# Why are toilets
# so good at poker?

**Cuz they always get a flush.**

# WHY DO GAS STATIONS CHARGE YOU TO FILL UP YOUR TIRES?

## INFLATION.

I took my dog to the beach the other day.

His name is Shark.

That
must have
gone well.

It didn't. Just imagine...
"Shark! Shark!
Come here, Shark!"

149

# MY DOCTOR SAID
# I WAS COLORBLIND.

## THAT DIAGNOSIS CAME OUT
## OF THE ORANGE.

# What did the triangle say to the circle?

**"You're pointless."**

# I have
# a really hard time
# getting to sleep.

**Really?**

**I can do it with**

**my eyes closed.**

I SPENT $80

ON A BELT

LAST NIGHT.

━━━━━ 👨 ━━━━━

MY GIRLFRIEND SAID
IT WAS A HUGE WASTE.

I was getting an Uber the other day. The driver said, "I love my job. I'm my own boss, and nobody tells me what to do."

Then I said, "Turn left here."

# I WAS AN
# UBER DRIVER ONCE.

**THEN I GOT FED UP WITH PEOPLE
TALKING BEHIND MY BACK.**

# NOTHING

## starts with an N
## and ends with a G.

**(It's true.)**

# WHAT DO YOU CALL A KNIGHT WHO IS AFRAID TO FIGHT?

## SIR RENDER.

# My wallet is just like an onion.

**Every time I open it, it makes me want to cry.**

# I DEBATED A FLAT-EARTHER ONCE. HE TOLD ME HE'D WALK TO THE EDGE TO PROVE ME WRONG.

I'M SURE HE'LL COME AROUND EVENTUALLY.

# Did you hear about the kidnapping at school?

It's okay—he woke up.

# WHAT GENERATION DOES FORREST GUMP BELONG TO?

**GEN A.**

# I wonder how a train hears another train coming.

**With its engineers.**

# WHAT DID THE JANITOR SAY WHEN HE JUMPED OUT OF THE CLOSET?

"SUPPLIES!"

# I wonder
# what country
# is growing
# the fastest?

**Ireland.**

**Everyday it's Dublin.**

# MY NEIGHBORS
# LISTEN TO GREAT MUSIC

## WHETHER THEY LIKE IT OR NOT.

My friends
and I put a
band together.
It's called
999 Megabytes.

We still haven't gotten
a gig though.

# I'VE ALWAYS BEEN ADDICTED TO THE HOKEY POKEY,

## BUT I TURNED MYSELF AROUND.

# I just brought chips
## to a salsa class.

## Huge misunderstanding.

A turtle was crossing the road when he got mugged by two snails.

When the police asked
him what happened,
he said, "I don't know.
It all happened so fast."

# WHAT DO ROBOTS DIP IN SALSA?

MICROCHIPS

# Which superhero likes hummus the most?

## Pita Parker.

# I GOT AN EMAIL EXPLAINING HOW TO READ MAPS BACKWARDS.

**IT WAS SPAM.**

# Yesterday
# a book just fell
# on my head.

I only had
my shelf to blame.

# My mom has forbidden me from making any more breakfast puns.

**She said if I do, I'm toast.**

# But dad keeps egging me on.

## He's such a ham.

# SOMEBODY JUST CALLED MY PHONE, THEN SNEEZED, COUGHED, AND HUNG UP.

## I'M GETTING SICK OF THESE COLD CALLS.

I've been starting to write my name in cursive.

It's now my signature move.

I WAS SO CONFUSED
LAST NIGHT WHEN
MY PRINTER STARTED
PLAYING MUSIC.

TURNS OUT IT WAS JUST JAMMIN'.

My friend said to me
the other day,
"You really have no
sense of direction,
do you?"

And I said,
"Where did that come from?"

**Tablets were replaced by scrolls, scrolls were replaced by books,**

186

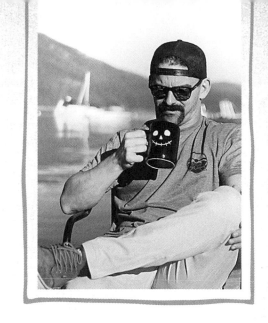

**and now
we just scroll
through books
on tablets.**

# DO YOU WANT TO HEAR A GOOD PIZZA JOKE?

## NEVER MIND, IT'S TOO CHEESY.

# I don't trust people who do acupuncture.

## They're back stabbers.

# People don't think grass be wet in the morning.

But it dew.

# Meet Logan Lisle

I love creating all kinds of content, but
I'm known for being a wedding videographer
in the Lake Tahoe, Reno, and San Diego areas.
I absolutely love what I do and have always had
a passion for creating a story from scratch.

I love Jesus.

I attended Bethel University, where I played
both football and baseball.

Trivia: One of my most popular TikTok
videos features a joke about Dr Pepper and
has gained more than 10 million views.